Be the Change

Be the Change

One Random Act of Kindness
at a Time

Neal C. Lemery

Neal C. Lemery

To those who serve their community through their compassion and love of others, and the many teachers who taught me to serve with kindness and empathy.

Published in the United States of America by Happy House Press, Tillamook, Oregon.
Author: Lemery, Neal C.

Summary: Do you want to make a difference? Do you want to change the world toward a kinder, happier place? Real change begins with one person, a person with the drive to change attitudes and behavior, towards a time of compassion and change. This book will empower you and inspire you to take charge, to be an effective innovator and leader for real change. Find your power to make a difference. Lemery's stories and examples offer you the tools, the inspiration to spread kindness, to truly be the change you want to see.

Be the Change: one random act of kindness at a time/ Neal C. Lemery – Happy house ed.

1. English language -- communities, social action. 2. Non-fiction essays. 3 Social science -- collective activism. 4. Community activism

Title. Be the Change: One Random Act of Kindness at a Time

E-book ISBN: 978-1-0880-6214-2 Trade paperback ISBN: 978-1-0880-6207-4
First Printing, 2022

Mentoring Boys to Men: Climbing Their Own Mountains (2015)

Homegrown Tomatoes: Essays and Musings From My Garden (2016)

Finding My Muse on Main Street (2018)(a novel)

Building Community: Rural Voices for Hope and Change: An Oregon Perspective (2020)

CONTENTS

OTHER BOOKS BY NEAL C. LEMERY   vii

Introduction   1

1 | Each of Us Can Be a Force for
Change   3

2 | Filling Up the New Calendar   7

3 | Reaching Out --- One to One   10

4 | Pruning Time   13

5 | Listening Can Be the Change   17

6 | How's the Family?   20

7 | Finding My Way   22

8 | The Power of Collective Silence   28

CONTENTS

9 | Guerrilla Gratitude --- Bringing Light Into Our World   31

10 | Being an Agent of Change   35

11 | Examining our Strengths and Weaknesses   39

12 | Our Differences and the Coming Change   43

13 | Taking On Change   48

14 | The Shirt Off My Back   54

15 | Taking Time to Grieve   59

16 | Recharging   63

17 | The Unexpected Conversation   66

18 | Roundabout: Struggling With Addiction   69

19 | Being the Healer: What Am I Here For   73

20 | Adapting to Change   77

CONTENTS

21 | Wanting Change: How Does That
Happen? 83

22 | Unexpected Gifts: Giving From the
Heart 86

23 | Happiness 89

24 | Simple Gifts 93

25 | Epilogue 96

ACKNOWLEDGEMENTS 97
ABOUT THE AUTHOR 98

Introduction

Each of us can make a difference to another person, to a group, and even the broader community.

That difference, that work of being an agent of change starts with one person – you.

This book is a collection of thoughts, expressions of optimistic intentions, to make a difference, to be a force to be reckoned with. I believe in the empowerment of one person to bring about fundamental change.

You and I can change attitudes and can help people reform their focus, their life force, to bring about basic, lasting change.

This work starts with one person who has a strong sense of idealism and purpose, who wants to make their life, and eventually, the world a better place.

That aspiration can be daunting, but it begins with one step, one small change. A person who is committed to an ideal and has a plan of action, is a force to be reckoned with, a game changer, and one of the most powerful forces in the world – a committed agent of change.

"Listen with curiosity. Speak with honesty. Act with integrity. The greatest problem with communication is we don't listen with curiosity, we don't listen with the intent reply. We listen for what's behind the words." Roy T. Bennett, *The Light in the Heart*   Onward!

1

Each of Us Can Be a Force for Change

We are in the midst of change. We've always been in transition, growing and evolving, but these times seem even more energized and challenging. Big challenges are all around us: the post-pandemic world, climate change, along with economic, social and political uncertainties. How many of us work and get an education, how we socialize, how we look at our world and our own expectations are in flux. How do we deal with all that?

I often don't handle change well. I like stability, predictability, the certainty that the demands of tomorrow will be comfortingly just like the demands of yesterday and today. But that's not realistic, and we are all compelled to adapt and move into uncharted and often uncomfortable new territory. I'll resist that, and want to stay in my rut, the old patterns and ways of navigating through life as comfortable as a pair of broken-in shoes.

Yet, I see that much does need to change. Like most of us, I'm conflicted, wanting some things to change, but then not wanting change. I struggle with that continuing conflict, that debate with myself about what needs to change and what we need to go back to or just stay with the status quo. After some inner conflict and self-talk, I mostly resolve those internal conflicts with myself by being a champion and voice for real reform, a recommitment to finding solutions, and doing things differently.

"It can be tempting to focus on all that is not working – the challenges, hurdles, and injustices. Good times can feel fleeting, like momentary distractions from the real work of life, which is more struggle and heartbreak than satisfaction and happiness." — Dan Rather

I'm dissatisfied in leaving the role of change maker, of rabble rouser, of being the dissenting voice that advocates new thinking, to the politicians, the theologians, and those who simply seem to be just wanting to make a lot of noise. All of us should take on that role, and raise the voice of the reformer, the change maker. As citizens, isn't that our duty? If I don't become the actor, the instigator, the loud voice, then don't I lose the right to complain?

"Change will not come if we wait for another person. We are the ones we've been waiting for. We are the change that we seek." — Barack Obama

My rants aren't just about political reform, about rewriting public policy and revitalizing our institutions to be the change makers. That work, and arguably the most important work, lies within ourselves and in the relationships we build in our communities. The work is one on one, deeply personal, and demanding of our own energies and skills.

The changes you and I can make can start with a conversation at the post office, with the gas station attendant, with a small group activity where we are deep in a community-building event. It can be seeing a need in the community for something and then taking leadership to fill that need. There is so much talent and passion in our community and it often becomes unleashed by the work of a single person. Often, it's not limited by money, but by our own willingness to step up and get something done. It requires our time.

The true power lies in the individual and the small group. "Never doubt that a small group of thoughtful, committed citizens can change the world. Indeed, it is the only thing that ever has." —Margaret Mead.

Want to change things up? Want to make a difference? Want to revitalize your community? Then have those encounters at the post office, the grocery store, the community event. Gather a group for coffee and have those deep conversations, the ones where everyone walks away with a to do list and a motivation to make some changes. Ask the tough questions, and seek out the meaningful conversations. Organize, motivate, daydream. Learn the skills you need to work on solutions.

Educate yourself. Imagine what may seem is impossible and take on those first few tentative steps. Be persistent, stubborn, and focused. Be outspoken, and speak your truth. Surround yourself with like-minded people and be determined. Know that you are called to leadership, to be the instrument of real change.

You will make a difference. You will be the change you want to see in the world.

2

Filling Up the New Calendar

The new calendar on the wall is fresh and clean. So far, there are only a few events are there. It is a fresh start to a new year.

The normal daily routine will return after all the winter holiday events come to an end. Life will soon begin filling up all that empty space. I'll miss the blissfully quiet winter evenings of the week between Christmas and New Year's, with shoes off, wrapped in a cozy blanket, with a good book and a cup of holiday tea. With the "to do" pre-holiday list mostly crossed off, I'm free to do what I darn well please, without a pressing agenda. It is a rare week of few expectations.

January and a new year are always filled with great promise and opportunity. I make a few resolutions, knowing that real change is possible, if I truly want to change and grow. I'm the one who gets to write on the calendar. Traditions and agendas are mine to follow, or change. It's my call. It is a time to claim my power.

I can grump and whine about the world and what our lives are like now. Or, I can do something about it. It starts with my attitude and where I decide to put my energy. That's intention, and I'm in charge of that. I have to want to intend to change what I don't like, and put myself into action.

When I point a finger at something, three of my fingers point back at me. I have more than a little responsibility for how the next year unfolds for me. When I demand accountability from others, I need to be looking in the mirror, to look at where most of my fingers point.

"Be the change you want to see," one of my inspiring role models, Mahatma Gandhi, said. I may not be able to change the world, but I can change who I am and how I live. I do have an impact on my little corner of the world. And in that, bigger changes can come. The work starts with me. That thought seems to be a universal truth.

What do I really want to see in this year? I need to figure that out, before I start to whine and mope about the world's state of affairs. First, change my attitude, find my intention, then develop my plan for achieving my goals, and fill up the calendar with all of my good, positive actions.

We live in community. Real change, real accomplishment only happens when there is a group that is engaged in that good work. Then there is engagement, ownership, and collective, community-focused achievement. Success comes from a collective effort, and is a community project, the energy coming from each of our individual intentions and acts, doing the work together.

One of Archbishop Desmond Tutu's favorite Zulu cultural values was *Ubuntu*. "One of the sayings in our country is *Ubuntu* — the essence of being human. *Ubuntu* speaks particularly about the fact that you can't exist as a human being in isolation. It speaks about our interconnectedness ... We think of ourselves far too frequently as just individuals, separated from one another, whereas you are connected and what you do affects the whole world. When you do well, it spreads out; it is for the whole of humanity."

I need to put more of his wisdom and determination to better society, and that spirit of *Ubuntu*, into my life and the life of our community.

The nearly empty calendar stares back at me, offering a challenge. I see opportunity and a challenge to move ahead in my life, and thereby change myself, my community, and the world, making it a more beautiful and creative place. There's work to be done. A lot of that empty space is ready for *Ubuntu*.

What's on your calendar?

3

Reaching Out --- One to One

I like the quiet of January. All the holiday activity ends, the decorations are put away, and the social calendar slows to almost nothing. There is clean, empty space, not only at home but in my life. It is time to breathe.

It is a time to be quiet, to connect with a friend, to have time for those serious and deep conversations that live deep in our hearts, to say what needs to be said and to put life in perspective.

The last few weeks have been marked by those quiet, almost sacred moments with someone close, to give some thinking time to a recent experience, or just getting to know myself better.

A friend who'd moved away a year ago unexpectedly showed up at a coffee shop where I was catching up with another friend. He crashed my time with my other friend, yet he clearly needed to talk. Moving and retiring from a long, demanding career had been hard for him, giving him a much-needed space to rest and to find himself. No longer identified by his job and his responsibilities, he was reconnecting with his wife and finding that he was enjoying life and putting together a new way of living. He was discovering he liked himself, that he enjoyed his friends, and he had a new purpose.

I listened, giving him space and time, being a friend. He needed to vent, to simply be heard. My time was a good present to offer him.

A while ago, I picked up a young man getting out of prison. He was making that life-changing drive from a prison cell to a half-way house. Two years "inside" had nearly snuffed out his soul. It was a long drive through beautiful, wide-open country with no bars or walls.

We talked of many things, me trying to be quiet, to listen to someone who hadn't had many people listen to him throughout his life.

We spotted a cormorant on a riverbank, drying its wings in the sunshine. He'd never seen a cormorant before and didn't know about their lives. We talked about freedom then, the freedom to fly, to fish on the river. Comfortable silences filled the rest of our trip, both of us finding our friendship quiet and easy. I thought of the healing power of solitude and nature, and the simple joy of sharing an experience with a friend.

I recently reconnected with a good friend, who reached out to me after one of her dear friends died by suicide. She had deep pain, and I was the ear she had sought. I listened; we cried. I gave the gift of listening, of not judging her friend, not advising her how to grieve, of not assuming or condemning. I held space for her, and acknowledged her pain.

We reconnected after the funeral, she wanting to talk about death and life and the hereafter, the messy mystery of what she was feeling and not easily understanding. I gave her time and permission to feel.

These quiet one on one conversations go both ways. Often, I need to be the talker and a friend be the listener. And, sometimes, it's looking at the stars or the waves on the beach, or picking my guitar all by myself, but knowing I'm not really alone.

I'm hoping I always have the time to reach out, or be the friend with the ready and willing ear and simply be there.

4

Pruning Time

The recent sunny weather gave me good reasons to get outside and start my early spring pruning chores. That work includes a lot of social and personal pruning, as well as the work in the garden. I have a long list, starting with eliminating some of the clutter and debris in my life, how the community can be improved, as well as taking a long look at the grapes that I had neglected to fully prune last year.

I'm motivated to sharpen my garden clippers, both literally and figuratively, because I'm seeing a lot of community pruning of our lives, our social institutions, and our daily work in these times of the pandemic. We are challenged by quarantines, other public health concerns and responding to economic challenges. Giving these community challenges a critical eye is a healthy step forward to improving our lives and having a positive response to these challenging times.

"Here we are, and what are we going to do about it?", a friend recently asked me, offering up a challenge.

The results of that pruning, that reorganization and revitalization are already apparent. Stagnant institutions are being revived, people are becoming more engaged, and new ideas are finding fertile ground. And, practices and attitudes that aren't helping to improve our lives are being pruned away, to the betterment of all of us. Community life is on a rebound.

As a gardener, I know that pruning away the dead, the diseased and the overlapping branches of plants improves their health, and stimulates them to be more vibrant, more productive plants. Pruning opens up a plant for more exposure to the sun, and is a proven way to invigorate older plants. I've recently learned that when I'm planting a shrub or tree, I should be also pruning the roots, which stimulates the plant and ensures its success in its new surroundings.

Such practices should be applied to our work in the community.

"In nature, every plant eventually is pruned in some manner. It may be a simple matter of low branches being shaded by higher ones resulting in the formation of a collar around the base of the branch restricting the flow of moisture and nutrients. Eventually the leaves wither and die and the branch then drops off in a high wind or storm. Often, tender new branches of small plants are broken off by wild animals in their quest for food. In the long run, a plant growing naturally assumes the shape that allows it to make the best use of light in a given location and climate. All one needs to do to appreciate a plant's ability to adapt itself to a location is to walk into a wilderness and see the beauty of natural growing plants." --- Douglas Welch.

I'm trying to apply those gardening principles to my own life by exploring new ideas, cleaning out some old time-wasting and stale activities and projects in my life, and finding new ways to improve our community life. Like any pruning job, my personal and community pruning involves taking a hard look at the structure, having a plan of what things should look like when I'm done, and getting tough on eliminating disease and the superfluous, the stuff that gets in the way of vigorous and fertile growth.

The thoughtful gardener takes the long view of where one's garden needs to be. By having a long-term vision, and taking some bold steps with one's clippers, as well as the occasional saw, transformation occurs. The needed change will soon produce obvious benefits, with the plant (and our community relationships) becoming healthier, more vibrant.

I struggle with change, and healthy pruning is one of the key tools we have to bring about needed growth in our relationships and our community. Recent stories in the **local on-line newspaper** and other media tell of how people are instigating change and revitalizing our community. We are taking on new ways of how we work, go to school, raise our kids, and care for each other. These changes are the subjects of deep and sometimes hard conversations. Yet, changes are coming. Indeed, many of them are already here.

I look around and see that I'm not the only one out in the yard with my clippers, pruning away the dead, the misshapen, the cluttered shrubs in the yard, and the parts of our social fabric that need revitalized. We gardeners are a persistent bunch, and recognize that pruning is an ever-present task on our to-do lists.

We can have sometimes heated discussions on how we should tend our community gardens, our institutions, and how we interact with each other. Our commitment to positive change, to effective pruning, is one of our great strengths, an aspect of our lives that we should celebrate with enthusiasm.

In those conversations, we can all grow and change, and become better gardeners of our community and our lives.

5

Listening Can Be the Change

When life gets chaotic and painful, I try to simply take a breath and become a better listener. Most of us don't feel like we are being heard, that our feelings and our own personal pain simply doesn't matter, that we are insignificant.

Being the active listener, using our attention and our ears, changes the dynamics and gives importance and compassion to those who haven't been heard, who feel ignored, unvalued. Our stories are powerful and liberating.

"We are made from the stories we've been told, the stories we tell ourselves, and the stories we tell one another. The world can be terrifying, wonderful, repulsive, wounding, comforting --- sometimes all at once. The stories we are fed often determine how we live in the contradiction." ---Mark Yakonelli, *Between the Listening and the Telling---How Stories Can Save Us* (2022).

Yakonelli is a professional listener, a collector of the deeply personal stories of others. A pastor and counselor, he helps others find their safe harbors and to share their lives. One of his tasks was to help Roseburg, Oregon heal from the devastation of the Umpqua Community College shooting in 2015. His work was to simply help create a safe place for people to share their pain, and to tell of their own courage and love of their community. He gave permission and sacred space for people to tell their stories, to express their innermost values and character. He helped heal a suffering community.

His book speaks of his own journey in gathering the stories of others and how that telling has changed himself and the communities he has visited. He continues to work with groups and individuals throughout the world, helping them to find their voices and to open their hearts.

"Stories can expand the boundaries of the heart to hold the chaos, the betrayals, the destructive absurdities with a sense of grace, resiliency, and moral courage. Or they can shrink us to become brittle, fearful, destructive. We need a comforting space and compassionate ears to sort out what we have suffered, to find the stories that recover and repair the world, to keep our hearts intact," he wrote.

In these times, I can often feel isolated. In spite of technology, I can easily feel lonely, disconnected from others. I can feel ignored. By sharing our stories, and by the simple act of telling my own story, bridges are built and connections with humanity and with community are made. We crave the good stories, the ones that reach into our hearts with a deep message of love and compassion, spreading empathy and good will.

There are many good listeners among us, the people who welcome us to share what is in our hearts, and to work on healing our pain. The Irish have a word for the people who do this work, *seanachie,* the story catchers.

As we go about our lives, and do the healing work that needs to be done in this world, we should pause and reflect on the healing power of story in the world, and the power that each of us has to be both the teller of stories and the listener.

6

How's the Family?

They are fine, thank God. I can't say that for my cousin, though, or my neighbor."

The line at the check stand fell silent, the clerk pausing in her work.

"That used to be such a casual question," she said. "Something you just said to get a conversation going. Now, that question goes to what's in my heart today."

Her eyes watered, and she wiped away a tear.

"I've lost a few relatives, my neighbor, and a couple of co-workers here," she said. "There's a lot of people I'm worried about, too.

The lady behind me, the one on the asking side of the question, took a deep breath and nodded.

"We're in hard times, and I'm so grateful for my health," she said. "But we don't talk much about what we are all going through, with all the loss, all the uncertainty."

"We have each other," the clerk said. "We need to care for each other, and talk about our pain, and the grief, and all the unknowing, the value of family and friends."

We looked at each other, nodding, smiling, sharing some deeply felt emotions that needed to be shared, realizing we were not merely in the grocery checkout, we were in sacred space and time.

The silence filled me up. I felt comforted, connected with people just like me --- scared, fearful, and lonely. I was with my tribe, my people, my community. Simply acknowledging all that jumble of feelings was what I had been needing.

The pandemic, the isolation, the sense of disconnectedness, it is all the elephant in our community living room. We are all going through this together, and sometimes, you just need to put that into words, get it out there, and share our hearts with each other. It is what community does the best, bringing us together in love and compassion.

7

Finding My Way

What should I be doing with my life?" a friend asked me the other day. I echoed the cliché about following your passion and left it at that. But that's not much of an answer. It was incomplete, and not respectful of a sincere question, one I still come across in my own life.

I recently read an essay about a young person's path of self-discovery, from an elementary school teacher, to musician, and now, reformed, changed up to a teacher of song writing and music.

"I don't recall any defining moment of decision to focus primarily on teaching music over performing it. I think it revealed itself in small steps, one choice at a time." (Avery Hill, What Does It Mean to Follow Your Passion? *Local Lore* newsletter, Portland Folk Music Society (Sept/Oct 2020).

She was reminded of Rilke's *Letters to a Young Poet* (1903): "I want to beg you, as much as I can ... to be patient toward all that is unresolved in your heart and to try to love the questions themselves ... Do not now seek the answers, which cannot be given to you because you would not be able to live them. And the point is, to live everything. Live the questions now. Perhaps you will then gradually, without noticing it, live along some distant day into the answer."

Avery says her songwriting "brings me closest to myself. By allowing myself deeper self-knowledge, I found I was able to follow the breadcrumbs from there. And I still am ---songwriting continues to allow me to stay centered and take whatever next step feels right."

"That said, I must admit, I squirm when anyone says: 'Follow your passion and you can make a living doing anything.' Clearly these folks underestimate the sheer amount of effort and dumb luck required to make this a true statement.

"Whatever your passion, go ahead. Follow it. By that I mean: be aware of what grounds you most, start there, and be flexible.

"What is the meaningful work in your life? What grounds you? Where do you feel most recognizable to yourself?' 'Live the questions,' as Rilke says, to which I add the path lies in asking them, not answering them."

My own roadmap through life is a series of questions and slogans, ones I come back to and reflect on in a quiet moment. I crave those small slivers of life I've tried to find for myself during the day, the ritual part of some of the disciplines and practices I've sought to establish for myself. Perhaps I, too, am trying to live the questions and not worry too much about having the right answers.

Part of my brain likes to see the world in terms of "either/or", a process of sorting out options in convenient, systemically ordered piles. What brings me joy? What doesn't bring me joy? Those questions, that approach to looking at life, can eliminate the boring, soul-killing tasks and obligations that don't advance what I value as good uses of my limited time on Earth.

I've been trying to be around my chosen family, who aren't usually the biological relatives. I want to avoid toxic people, their poisons often putting me down, diminishing me, which is often a slow chipping away of my goodness, my purposeful direction. Knowing that I can choose my family and friends liberates me and expands my potential. I strive to be a better manager of "family time" and take nourishment from those who enrich me and challenge me to excellence.

I'm an advocate for finding purpose and meaning in life through service to others. I try to reach out and practice small acts of kindness and charity. I work on my empathy and my self-actualization through kindness, volunteerism, and my creativity. Even a few minutes of gardening, picking up a piece of trash, or saying a few kind words to someone at the coffee shop or the store are forms of service and community building. You change experiences and attitudes, and bring the proverbial ray of sunshine into an encounter. Your attitude can be contagious and transformative.

Another dichotomy in my life is to decide to act either out of fear or out of love. I can cringe through life, my sword in hand, obsessed with seeing the world as a disaster waiting to happen, my role in it as the continual failure, fulfilling my expectations as one who is inadequate and "no good". Or, I can flip that, seeing the world and my experiences as acts of love, as possibility to do good, and to advance the values and ethics that I cherish, and build a better world. That work always starts in my little corner, with my own two hands and my own heart and voice. Words and small acts of kindness do make a difference, and become the tools of my trade, a builder of a better world.

When I have a clear intention, good actions follow from that.

I strive to be my own best friend, being kind to myself, helping myself across a busy street, or sitting with myself in a challenging situation, offering myself comfort and solace. I can be an advocate for myself, a calming presence, a voice of reason and support, and offer myself a big hug and a shoulder to cry on. I can pull out the handkerchief and lovingly wipe away the tears. Those are transferable skills to be present with others, but I often benefit from practicing that good work on myself.

I practice self-care. I'm my own best nurse. I can plump up my pillow, put on the extra blanket, make myself some comfort food and find my teddy bear at the end of a hard day.

The idea of "holding space" for others, by simply being present and attentive, also applies to me. The rest of the world's insanity can be swirling around me, which is a reminder for me to hold some space for myself and be self-caring, to be the caretaker.

I do best at problem solving when I can see the Truth. Truth is often elusive, and others who seem to want to do harm to me, or use me, take my time and money, will manipulate the truth, bending and distorting it to their own advantage. I'm prone to be a people pleaser, and default to thinking that others are always genuinely caring and kindly with me. But, that action by others is often manipulation and deceit. It really is my task to know what is the truth, and to recognize deception and truth bending for what it is, a means of lying and fraud. In that truth seeking, I need to hold my own self to the fire, to be self-critical, evaluative, assessing. I need to be aware of my own self-talk, my own ways I sabotage myself. It is a question of self-actualization, self-esteem, honoring and valuing my own friendship with myself. It becomes self-advocacy and self-assessment, self-love.

I need to see myself as unique, special, one of a kind. I do best when I deeply discount other people's opinions about me. What others think of me really has nothing to do with me. They are caught up in their world, and their thoughts about me only help them explain their own perceptions of themselves, their own belief system. They don't really know me anyway, especially the part of me that is the precious, unique parts of my soul that are God's special gifts to me. The judgments of others are simply opinions, and really are uninformed opinions, not based upon Truth. My own value, my own place in this world really is none of their business.

I try to declutter my life. That can start with things, but that work becomes especially effective in managing my relationships and encounters with the world. It goes back to the "does it bring me joy?" question.

There's also the "three gates" approach for managing what comes out of one's mouth: is it true, it is necessary, is it kind?

I'm a verbal guy, opinionated and outspoken. I share my opinions, probably too freely. I've been trying to apply the "three gates" practice in my interactions with others. I'm trying to tamp down the judgmental aspects of what I say, and apply these "filters". In that, I am working on being a better listener, and actually welcoming the times of quiet, of being present, and holding space for others.

8

The Power of Collective Silence

I found myself at a local café, having a late breakfast, with about a dozen other community members who had the same idea. At a nearby table, a family was enjoying themselves, highlighted by the smiles and laughter of their sweet six-month-old baby.

As babies are wont to do, laughter turned into cries and wails, filling the busy café with sounds of distress. Mom quickly responded by picking up the baby and cuddling it, as good parents do.

The man at the counter turned towards the family, a look of disgust and anger on his face.

"You need to take him outside and give him something to cry about. He needs a good spanking for acting that way," he said, his booming voice reverberating throughout the room.

In an instant, the room fell into a deep and pregnant silence. Every eye turned towards the angry man, every face stony and silent. Nothing was said, the only sound now the quiet murmurs of the now-again content baby.

My mind whirled, part of me wanting to stand up and give the man a piece of my mind, the idiocy of violence, the long-lasting impact of what we euphemistically call "corporal punishment," and the rudeness of strangers interjecting their values on a young family who were simply out for a good time with their child.

Slapping, spanking, the mentality of "giving you something to cry about", pushed a lot of my emotional buttons, bringing back bad memories in my own life, both personal and professional. I well knew the impact of that kind of thinking on family members and friends, and how those traumatic experiences often profoundly impact us for the rest of our lives.

No one said a word, even the cook stopping her work at the stove, as we all glared at the man, until he finally turned back in his seat and took a sip of his coffee. A long minute passed, until the baby laughed a little and we all resumed our lives, until we all realized something important was being said in the silence.

It was a good minute, a minute of both rebuke for a really bad idea and a time to reflect on how we should deal with kids, what they need from the rest of us.

It gave me pause to reflect on whether I should have launched into my lecture to the man about the evils of violence and the messages that sends to kids. The silence gave me time to again realize that my well-rehearsed rant on using violence and anger to raise a child would have likely fallen on deaf ears, that the man wouldn't be changing his thinking because of what I was going to tell him. I was reminded of the power of collective silence, and I felt that power reverberate through the café.

If he was going to change his thinking, that would come at a different time, in a different place, when he was ready to really hear what he had said, and how he looks at the world, and how he learns about his community's values.

Instead, the community at that café spoke a bigger message, in that big, beautiful collective silence of disapproval and disgust. Mere words wouldn't have been nearly as effective as our group effort to turn our heads towards the man, and simply be silent.

Conversations resumed, and the man kept being ignored. The waitress didn't refill his coffee, and slapped down his check beside his empty cup. He left his money and slipped out the door, not daring to utter another word.

I often overestimate the value of a well-turned phrase, or what I might think is a polished, professional writing on a particular issue. Sometimes, it is in the silence that we truly hear the words of wisdom, the message we want to send, the message we need to hear.

9

Guerrilla Gratitude ---
Bringing Light Into Our World

Any act, any kind word, is capable of making a change for the better in our world. Each of us has so many opportunities to make it a better place. A few kind words at the grocery store or post office, a simple act of kindness to help someone along in their day, maybe a cheery note or a phone call. It can all make a difference.

I was in a hurry last week as I came into my favorite coffee shop, intent on getting to work on what I thought was an important project, one that couldn't wait.

I pulled open the coffee shop door, focused on ordering my coffee. I nearly ran over a woman holding two cups of coffee and looking stressed. I looked behind her, seeing her frail mother, struggling with her cane and trying to keep up with her daughter.

It was time to pause and show a little kindness. I pulled the door fully open and held it for them, letting the woman with the two hands of coffees navigate outside, as she offered her arm to her mother. They shuffled out the door, both of them thanking me, and breaking into smiles. I muttered "no problem," and smiled back.

It was time for me to take a breath, admire the beauty of the fall day; time for some gratitude. The world had given me an opportunity to be kind, make people happy and take care of the community.

The opportunities continued. A couple had followed me in, seemingly in a hurry to get their coffee and resume their journey. I stepped back, letting them have first place in the queue for the barista. The man gave me a funny look, like I was doing something strange, out of the ordinary.

"No problem," I said. "I'm taking it easy today." I repeated the smiles I'd received from the mother and daughter, and felt my day brighten.

He just nodded, likely not knowing how to respond. There was a lesson or two there. At least, a lesson for me, taking time to let things unfold, to be part of an accommodation in someone's day, making things go easier. But, I got my reward: a nod, perhaps a sense of someone being kind and gracious to them, maybe some reflection on what the day was about.

I'd assumed they were on vacation, which is hopefully a time for some rest, a pause from the routine of daily life, and simply enjoying a sunny fall day in a beautiful place, topped off with some great coffee. The least I could do for them was to be kind.

My coffee shop punch card was filled by my usual order, and I gave it to the barista, asking them to use it to treat the next person who would come through the door. I've been reading a book about "guerrilla gardening", where you surreptitiously add beauty to public space. Perhaps this is "guerrilla gratitude". We can all be rebels with a cause.

When I checked in at a hospital last week for some lab work, a very kind man gently and efficiently guided me through the process, even walking me over to the lab and then guided me to my next appointment. He was extraordinary. Yet for him, it seemed just an ordinary day, just doing his job. He made my wife and me laugh and feel at ease, as he went about his work. His saintliness was just what I needed, calming my anxiety and frenzy.

Other employees were also extraordinarily kind and helpful, bringing to me an atmosphere of gentleness, welcoming, and professionalism. You could tell they loved their work and were proud of their competence, knowing they were saving lives. It was nice to see that a large organization doing important work appreciated great customer service.

"If you light a lamp for someone else, it will also brighten your path," said Buddha. We need to be a society of lamplighters, and not keep our compassion and kindness hidden away. It is the treasure we need to share.

Life, real life, a good life, is really about kindness and accommodation and patience. Life is paying it forward, diffusing the crisis of the moment, and quietly getting things done and put in order. The cost is really non-existent. A little time, perhaps a few more minutes spent with someone, some kind words, a few deep breaths, and exuding calmness and service to others. We get that back, at least tenfold, in our lives.

I keep re-experiencing those lessons, and the need to be patient and kind, both on the giving and the receiving parts of life. Such wisdom bears repeating, along with a whole lot of doing, part of "guerrilla gratitude".

10

Being an Agent of Change

Change can occur in many ways and take many forms. Change begins with me, from the inside out. I am in charge. Change is my choice, as is the direction of the change one wishes to instigate and encourage.

Empowering myself is my choice and serves me, at my direction and within the scope of my intention and my purpose. This work implies that one has a plan.

"Vision without action is a daydream. Action without vision is a nightmare." — Japanese proverb.

"A seed grows with no sound but a tree falls with huge noise. Destruction has noise but creation is quiet. This is the power of silence ... grow silently." — Confucius.

We all can make a lot of noise. At the end of the day, are we just left with the noise, or have we advanced? Have we made a difference? Is the world a better place, at least our tiny little corner of the world?

Fundamental, course-correcting change comes deep from within ourselves. It is soul work, spiritual in nature. To be a change maker, you need intention, a plan, and passion. Deep inside of one's self, there needs to be a fire burning, hot enough to forge the steel of one's ideas into tools for effective and lasting change.

This work requires a deep commitment to perseverance: pure unadulterated stubbornness.

An aspect of change is the support or creation of a habitat in which change can occur.

Partial habitat is, perhaps, a more realistic objective, when you are working towards change. It is a place for kindness and creativity to take root and thrive. Perhaps I cannot fashion a perfect world, ideal in all its values and aspirations. Perhaps I can't change people's thinking or their perspectives. Creating a complete, whole habitat is very often beyond my abilities. Yet, I can work towards that, doing some of the essential work.

I can help create a change in how we live, where we grow and learn, and interact with one another. It may not look like much, from the outside. A quiet spot, space for contemplation or a quiet conversation, an oasis in the chaos and tumult of daily life. And maybe only one or two people come to this place and find some peace, some space to be calm and reflective, or to create somethings from their thoughts and intentions. Maybe such work is not consciously done and this space not even consciously noticed or felt, even on a deep, almost invisible level.

It is enough that such a place exists and is available. There is an intention present and available for others. It is enough that I have intention and hold space in my mind and in my life. I can move forward to act to have such an opening — a place even metaphysically, where there can be rest, contemplation, a pausing of frenzy and daily life. There can be space to regroup, reassess, re-evaluate, and relaunch.

There are many forms of a partial habitat. Perhaps it takes the form of a poem, a painting, a song, a spot in a garden, even the sharing of a cup of coffee with a friend, or a casual conversation in a public place. Perhaps it is the holding of space for someone, an honoring of something beautiful, even the expression of one's intention.

Partial habitat is a respite from the mundane, the cataclysmic, the overwhelming demands of the world. The creating of this space is, perhaps, the least I can do in this life to advance my purpose for my existence, the fulfillment of the tasks for me assigned by the Creator.

My destiny, if you will, is to be a force for change, for improving this world --- at least this culture. Positive energy and positive effort, a being of part of the shift of cultural and social propulsion creating something new.

Change is inevitable. Change is part of our nature, our very essence. Growing and improving how we relate to each other, how we live our lives and fulfill our purpose, our mission in this life is elemental, fundamental to being human.

Being a force for change is what we are here for. When we are gone from here, that life-force, that energy will be what we will be remembered for. That work is a way of affirming our inner goodness.

It can also be a rejection, a turning away of values and expressions that are contrary to our values and our moral stands. Such resistance, such affirmation of our own true and honest values and thoughts are statements of our own principles, our own voices for our ideals.

This work is advocacy: advocacy for humanity, for progress, for being an instrument of change. This work is fundamental to both our own humanity and our sense of self, and our self-worth. Self-actualization, self-reliance, self-fulfillment — these are my bucket list items now.

Making a difference, even however slight or even minimal, is a planting of a seed. We really don't know when that seed will sprout and what will be the result of that germination. We plant anyway, sensing a eternal optimism, a sense of home and promise for better days ahead.

11

Examining our Strengths and Weaknesses

Whenever we come together to share strengths it breeds competition; whenever we come together sharing our weaknesses, it breeds community." — Anonymous

We live in divisive times. If one spends much time "catching up" on news or social media or talking about politics and social trends with one's friends, the common theme seems to focus on our divisions, our differences, and winning some argument or political event. We like to boast about our strengths and hide our weaknesses.

But life isn't about winning or losing, or "us vs them". Our sporting events, which we support because we want something fun and wholesome for ourselves and our kids, often is analyzed in terms of win/lose. We like to measure strength and power. We keep score, and often that seems to be the primary reason for the activity and our attention we pay to it. Even the supposedly non-partisan, individually focused "pure sport" Olympic Games are reported complete with scorecards of national medal awards.

Discussions and viewpoints on political and social issues are often laced with mean comments and foul language, often thinly disguised with code words. We are encouraged to laugh with comedians who can make the most acidic standup routines, which we still refer to as comedy.

Informed and well-reasoned political conversation and a willingness to look at another point of view often is not on most of our social agendas for the day. Some politicians seem to want to advance their careers by acting with meanness and spite. They act as destroyers, not leaders of social advancement.

If everyone is now keeping score and arguing only for the sake of arguing, rather that persuading or informing, what is the grand prize? What are we attempting to gain? Is there a national championship for the loudest, most shrill argument? Are there extra points to be gained for sheer meanness? Does the winner get invited to the White House and be able to scream their point of view to a national audience? Or have I missed the news of a parade down Broadway, with a tickertape parade of nasty vitriolic social media posts?

Such tactics don't change anyone's opinion, and, I suggest, not much learning occurs, nor do we advance the common welfare.

The gentle, collaborative model of social life is more fruitful. I do see a new feeling of cooperation, of coming together to advance both individual and social goodness. I see volunteers everywhere, building up people, providing educational opportunities. There are small flickers of great and unselfish actions.

My neighborhood now has several "educational pods" where parents and friends are providing private schooling for kids of all ages. There is laughter and enthusiasm, and the occasional gaggle of kids out for a jog between classes, satisfying their P.E. requirements for the day. Families are deeply involved in their kids' education, with small classes and individual attention, coupled with virtual learning, allowing kids to benefit from a variety of learning styles and curriculum.

Small businesses are experimenting with a wide range of business models, and many workers are working from home, either part or full time, allowing them to be productive and have quality time with family, without the expense and exhaustion of a long commute to work. There is serious discussion about the role of our traditional routines of work and career models.

Virtual learning isn't for all situations, but it has found a place in my life, allowing me to participate in and dabble in a variety of activities and experiences. I've been able to benefit from a rich selection of broadcasted art performances and educational presentations. We still need the in-person connections and the "juiciness" of one on one conversations and socializing, but there are some welcome advantages to this post-pandemic world.

The world now has amazing tools for communication and improving our lives. Miraculous innovations and discoveries are commonplace. We can accomplish so many tasks. Yet, humanity's hunger for power, wealth, and status slows our efforts to improve the lives of all. Why we allow that to occur is an urgent question for all of us.

I suggest this paradox between what we can accomplish and what is done is essentially an ethical and spiritual challenge. What is humankind's purpose? What are we alive to do?

In that quest, that work to answer these deep questions challenges our approaches to achieving a meaningful future. Coming together to take on our weaknesses builds our community.

12

Our Differences and the Coming Change

We are emerging into new times, new opportunities. How are we going to take advantage of all of the possibilities? The end of the pandemic restrictions is not going to be a return to normal, "the way it was". So much has changed, and we are challenged to adapt, to take the lessons learned, and to move ahead into our changed society.

No longer is education only going to be based on in-person learning. Many of our work environments now embrace working from home. We are adapting to a variety of virtual learning, work, and participatory experiences, allowing us to be productive in so many ways. We are no longer constrained by geography, but rather by our ability to take advantage of the many ways we can interact, to learn, and to produce value in our lives.

We have rediscovered the importance of personal relationships, and the value of social interactions at every level.

Children in my neighborhood joyfully interact in small groups, guided by parents and neighbors who have become experienced in the teaching arts. Educators are seen again as masters, gifted in the rearing of our kids. Students are able to access a variety of learning styles and are discovering how they can better acquire and master the knowledge they need in this changing world.

Now, we cherish social interactions and the benefit of collaboration and access to public health services. Health care has greatly advanced in the last several years, incorporating the principles of evidence-based research and the development of preventative measures, such as vaccines and universal access to new treatments and methodologies. We have been reminded of the benefits of access to quality health care.

We now plainly see the benefit of community-wide access to the internet, and how each child, each adult, benefits from both technology and one-on-one teaching.

"If there is going to be change, real change, it will have to work its way from the bottom up, from the people themselves. That's how change happens." — Howard Zinn.

We need to take advantage of all of these changes, and the challenges that have forced us to re-evaluate how we've managed in the past, and how we want to live in the future. It is up to us, from the grass roots up. My renewed interest, thanks to the pandemic, in gardening, baking, and in communicating one on one with friends and family on a deep level, has made me more connected, more involved, and more attentive to what really matters in my life, as well as the life of our community. I see technology as a tool to advance my humanity, and not the end result of my use of it.

We've learned that the social institutions and customs that really work, that really improve lives, deserve our attention and require our energies so that they can thrive. And, the old ways and institutions that don't serve their purposes anymore, need to be left behind, making room for what does work, what really makes a difference.

We've learned that the personal touch, going the extra mile with someone, in an intimate and sensitive approach, is profoundly effective. There's a rise in entrepreneurship and ingenuity.

Creativity is blossoming and is finding room in our changing economy. In that, our true core values are being honored and advanced. Individual talents are being nurtured and admired. Quality family time is seen as essential to a happy life and a productive society.

We are now surrounded by lessons in collaboration. Our differing observations and opinions are really just different expressions of our many common values. Our vocal, often strident debates on what we think are fundamental differences, are really just conversations on how best to advance our common community values: the power of meaningful choices, the value of an individual's contributions, that differing viewpoints can advance the common good, that a person's individuality, their uniqueness, is a highly cherished asset to society.

We have more in common than our divergent, often strident, views. We're learning the lessons of being good listeners and learning from a different point of view. From those conversations, we can move closer to finding the truth, and taking action steps that truly address the problems we all face. We need to keep asking "what is the common good?"

If we look at our differences as a process of education and personal growth, and to truly strive for finding the truth in a choppy sea of propaganda and misinformation, we all can work towards improving society, and having respectful, meaningful debates. Each of us needs to be less attached to the idea that only I know the truth, only I am the holder of the correct answer. Then we can truly be lifelong learners and be part of the solutions, be an agent of positive change.

A healthy democracy requires that we take less ownership in what we think is the unbridled truth and be willing to accept that there is more to learn, there is more to be discovered. And, perhaps, I can even admit that I don't know all the answers, that the real truth is awaiting all of us in this journey. This awareness of the dangers of ego-based opinion holding is one of our big lessons from these challenging times. These are good lessons our kids need to learn from us.

Technological advancement is now being seen as not the end result of our labor, the "end all and be all" but as a toolbox to further our human values, our relationships, and as a way to provide even more opportunities for learning and happy lives. We are learning that technology is not our master, but our servant.

And the good change, the needed change, comes from each of us. We've all been in school these last several years, learning and relearning some of the basic lessons in life, and contemplating the wisdom of some of our beliefs and our institutions. If we act differently, then our lives can be changed, hopefully for the better.

We have learned that if we want things to be different now, we are the agents of change. We have to know where we want to go, what needs to be different. We need to do the work, and to make the changes that need to happen. It is up to us.

13

Taking On Change

The pandemic was a time of postponement, not taking care of business. Life has had a lot of waiting around, and my frustration and impatience show up in high numbers on my emotional dashboard. The personal "to do" list seems to keep growing and has few check offs.

In normal times, my life's challenges usually get resolved with me realizing it is a time to change. And that work to refresh is always so productive and satisfying. In these times, much of what we are facing seems out of my grasp to change. Most things get booted down the road. Like the virus, procrastination has often become the new normal.

I often escape into my music. I pick up my guitar and find some solace, literally tuning out the world. Even there, there is a need for change. In guitar speak, it is realizing it is time to restring my faithful six string acoustic.

There's a lifespan for good steel guitar strings. All my chord making, strumming and picking literally wears out the wires, as well as providing proof of my labors with bigger callouses on my fingertips. In that playing, oil and dirt from my fingers are rubbed into the strings. My picking and the vibrations become tiresome to the guitar (and probably the rest of my household).

I play my guitar for its mellowness, harmonizing tones and its predictability in terms of the sounds that are emitted, consistent with one's repetition of chord patterns, strumming, and finger picking. One gets to mix it up, of course, by using different sizes and materials for strings, and the qualities that are unique for each guitar.

Other variables are at play: the type and age of the wood, the thicknesses of materials, the design, humidity, and how precise you are in tuning each string. You add other variables, too: the methods and styles of finger picking, flat picking and slides, plus little touches like pull offs, hammer ons, and chiming; not to omit the likely dozens of other techniques and styles I've yet to hear about, let alone begin to attempt. Guitars become "sweeter" with age, the wood conditioned by time and playing to evolve into an even more expressive instrument. It is a metaphor that I appreciate more the older I get.

Yet, it all goes back to having strings in good shape. It really is the simple things that make a big difference in how my guitar sounds in a day. Aside from all the complexities and sophistication of the accomplished musician, it is the act of restringing and putting on a set of new strings that makes my guitar come alive again. Sometimes, you just need to get rid of the rust and dirt and the "worn out" aspects of life.

I procrastinate, doubting myself that it really might be time to change the strings. I'm good at the kind of self-talk that talks me out of making a needed change. I'll bargain with myself, offering excuses like time, or effort, or thinking it really hasn't been that long since I put on the strings that are there now. I ignore the principle of guitar strings that age and wear out are a function of how much you play, versus what the calendar might say.

It's not like I have to run down to the music store for a set, or that the cost will break my budget. For all their magic, guitar strings are a bargain. I almost always have on hand good to high quality strings, engineered for a long and vigorous life, with promises of crispness and high-quality tones. And, I have all the little tools, wood cleaners, and the other gizmos of the specialized world of guitar string replacement. I learn by trial and error in my music. My string changing regimen is a product of years of redoing and reliving most every mistake you can make, plus having some exciting adventures along the way.

Today, for instance, was the reliving of the occasional crisis of having a wooden peg pop out and plummet into the depths of the guitar box. These little pegs, which I want to think are insignificant, are really essential. They secure the little "ball" end of the string snug in the hole in the body of the guitar. They grasp one end of the string, so you can then tighten it, eventually giving enough tension on the string that it will be tightly in place, that it will vibrate and produce a note, fully a part of the guitar.

When pegs run wild, I feel helpless and inept, adding salty language to the experience. The peg then plays hide and seek, rattling around the inside, and getting caught in nearly every crevice of the various wooden bracings inside. I do the dance, holding and shaking the upside-down guitar in every angle and configuration, hoping to maneuver it to come out of its cave and rejoin its companions on the face of the guitar. There is the added chance of having the peg flying through the air and lodging under the nearest piece of furniture, prolonging the chase. More excitement comes when the cat decides to help.

This game is sometimes played with a guitar pick. My personal record for chasing the reluctant and shy guitar pick inside the guitar is a (now) laughable three weeks. At best, the usual plastic pick is worth, maybe fifty cents, but still, it's the principle of the matter and a personal challenge. Man vs guitar pick. I WILL prevail.

The string changing ritual offers other challenges, such as squinting sufficiently in order to thread the thin wires through the holes in the tuner pegs at the other end of the guitar, so you can then wrap the wires around the pegs and begin to tighten them. The shiny wires blend in well with the chrome tuner pegs. In this stage, it is easy to qualify for a Purple Heart for Guitarists, by giving yourself a substantial poke in the finger. My guitar is frequently sanctified by my sacrificial efforts, accompanied by that now well used salty language.

You have to put the strings on in the right order, of course. Each string has a different diameter, with lower notes produced by thicker strings. That seems simple and logical. But, we're talking me and mechanical tasks. Disasters can occur, with a brand-new string in the wrong place that's tightened too much, accompanied by the unexpected loud twang of a broken string. Then there's that deep feeling of ineptitude. Another box of strings is now on the table, adding to the potential confusion. I've learned to practice rituals of how I lay out the paper string packets and the manage the order of installation, much like a priest officiating at a high mass.

It is even more fun with a 12 string guitar. String changes on a 12 string increase the challenge by several magnitudes of difficulty, where the rubric requires the lowest four pairs (courses) to be tuned in octaves, but the top two courses are tuned in unison on the same note. Doubling the number of strings and the number of pegs that can go wild more than doubles the fun.

As one hits the home stretch, with all six new strings in place, you get a sense of impending success. When you finish up the tuning ritual with the electronic tuner and the seemingly never ending turning of the pegs on the tuner machines, the transformed guitar begins to sing its songs with a fresh, much improved voice. New strings stretch, so the need to retune is accelerated. I'm always struck by the sweetness of the new strings.

"Wow, I should have changed these long ago. The new ones sound great," I usually proclaim to the household, causing my wife to mutter that I always say that when I put on new strings. Still, it is continually a fresh and delightful discovery, each and every time. I am, perhaps, a slow learner.

I coil up the old strings, and attempt to put them in the garbage can, along with the handful of snipped off string ends, from both the old and new sets. This tangle of wires always resists me, usually breaking free and uncoiling onto the kitchen floor, attempting to evade my thick-fingered efforts to corral them and restuff them into the can. After all our quality time together, they just don't seem to want to leave. It can be another perilous time for exposed fingers and toes, another opportunity to earn a Purple Heart for Guitarists. Now, though, I can see them in all their dirt and grime, the finish worn off and dull, any new effort to bring forth any decent sound doomed to failure. Tired and worn out, they are ready for a rest.

The rules and the pleasures of guitar string changes applies to other parts of my life, as well. I learn a lot from this occasional task. Familiar jeans well past their prime and faded, torn t-shirts and flannel shirts, with ripped sleeves, deserve similar replacements. Shoes, however, are the worst. I can easily wear out a pair of my favorite hiking shoes, my daily attire, until every last aspect of padding and support are long gone. A new pair tells me immediately that the old shoes were at least several months past their lifespan, and that familiar phrase again crosses my lips, "I should have changed these a long time ago.".

These discoveries can be applied to other aspects of my life: toothbrushes, cracked glassware, chipped plates, bent forks, even one's favorite chair. I can apply these lessons to my community life, as well: overly familiar places to hang out and tiresome, sometimes toxic people who refuse to grow in their thinking and experiences.

My guitar teaches me a lot about life: perseverance, consistent practicing, having a regular time to focus on some quality "me time". And, change.

We can wake up in the morning, engage the world, and remark to everyone within ear shot, "I should have changed this a long time ago."

14

The Shirt Off My Back

A familiar phrase we often use is that someone would give the shirt off their back to help someone else. Last week, that became reality for me and a young man, as we drove away from the prison where he'd been the last two and a half years. Our destination was a halfway house, where he could restart his life, find a job, and be a productive citizen. He has big plans: vocational school, a job, long hikes in the woods, a family someday.

Some will argue that the hardships and obstacles facing a parolee is part of his "punishment", that one shouldn't do the crime if you can't do the time. Felons don't deserve our kindnesses, and should be treated as the scum that they are. They deserve their hardships, and it is their lot in life.

I suppose those attitudes are easy to come by, and that the life of those getting out of prison is low on many people's priorities and compassion. Perhaps, until you get to know a person, and hear their story, until you match the face with the stories they tell of their lives.

"Lock 'em up and throw away the key" and the problem will go away. Right?

Well, those men and women will return to society, join the workforce, and will have family and friends, just like everyone else. How they go about their lives, and the decisions they make, is fundamentally shaped by the resources they have when they walk out of the prison gates.

My young friend left prison the other morning with only a pair of pants, a sweatshirt, and shoes provided by the prison. No underwear, no socks, no coat, and no cash in his pocket. His life savings, including the federal stimulus money (which we all received last year) was in a check. Of course, he has no bank account, no ID except a prison issued ID card. His lost driver's license hadn't been replaced.

He has an Oregon Trail food stamp card, but of course, he needed a phone to activate that. Yep, you guessed it. He had no phone. His family could have shipped him a phone that he could have picked up at his release that morning, but the prison never told them about that option.

The check for his money was $300 short. The prison had decided to fine him for a rule infraction last week, and took away his inmate phone privileges on top of that.

We headed off to a city four hours away, to see his probation officer, and to check in at the halfway house. He wasn't sure where his new home was, or what it looked like.

He got out at dawn, when the sweatshirt kept him warm. Later on, it warmed up and he started to sweat. He put on a determined face, not wanting to complain to me. No one else had offered to pick him up and make the trip with him, so I was the only way to get him where he needed to go.

"Do you have anything else to wear?" I asked, knowing the answer as all his worldly possessions were loosely piled in a cardboard box in the back seat of my truck.

I'd needed to do an overnight trip to pick up my friend, due to the early morning release time, so I had a few clothes in my suitcase. I dug out a shirt I'd bought for myself a few weeks ago, and gave it to him.

"Oh, no, I can't take that," he said.

But I insisted and he managed a smile as he slipped it on. It was soft, colorful and new, something he hadn't experienced in the last few years. He looked away at the changing landscape, filled with fields, trees, far away mountains, and blue sky, things he hadn't seen in his life for too long of a time. A tear rolled down his cheek, and I looked away, concentrating on my driving, and giving him some quiet time. A tear fell onto my face, too, being reminded of simple things, and how so much in life I take for granted.

What I call Freedom Day is sacred space, where emotions often too intense to comprehend fill one's heart. Often, there are no words, only tears and hugs.

We stopped along the way a few times — fabulous coffee in a small town's only coffee shop, breathing fresh air at a roadside rest area overlooking a display of bright fall leaves and a river. As we took in the serenity of the river, we found no words to speak. He turned to me and embraced me, his hug saying it all.

I parked outside of the probation office, waiting for my friend to complete his check in, and finding out where he was going to live. I watched a drug deal go down across the street, and the parade of customers going to the nearby pot shop, some of whom had just left the probation office.

He settled into his new home, and the staff introduced themselves to me. Good, deeply committed people, being kind and hospitable, as we settled my friend in, making his bed, finding out where the bathroom and the kitchen were.

"This will be fine," he said. "I'll be OK."

He walked me to my truck. It was time to say goodbye. It had been a good day, good conversations, a trip of amazing natural beauty, and peace, a deepening friendship. And freedom.

I slipped into Dad Mode, giving him one last hug, and a short sermon of Dad Advice, giving him one last dose of love, encouragement, and fatherly advice.

"I don't have any money," he reminded me, hesitation catching in his voice. We'd had a talk earlier about his lack of funds, and I'd promised to spot him some cash, something to carry him through until he could get to the bank. I apologized for forgetting my commitment, and dug out my wallet.

"That's too much," he said, but I wouldn't take any back.

"Take yourself out for coffee," I said, and added another twenty.

"Here's your shirt," he said. He started to unbutton it.

"That's your shirt now," I said. "It's part of our deal, part of what we needed to do today."

I got in my truck and drove down the street, lowering the window to give him one last wave. In the rearview mirror, I saw him wave back, and wipe away something on his face. A few tears wetted my face, and I gulped down what would have been a full-blown sob session.

The road home was quiet. I was lost in my thoughts. This wasn't the first time I'd taken a young man from what we call "correctional institutions" to a fresh start. Freedom Day, I call it. And, sadly, the stories run together. The lack of clothes, the cardboard box of possessions, the lack of financial care, the uncertainty of where they will spend the night and the next few months of their lives. There's the scarcity of family, too, and that points back to understanding why they were locked up to begin with.

I've read where the cost of housing one prisoner in our state prison system is close to $60,000 a year, and that mental health services, vocational training, and transitional housing are often the first to be cut. My friend needs all of that. The system isn't dealing with his depression, PTSD, and anxiety, not to mention his alcohol and drug issues, those necessities somehow not part of his life in prison, not part of his parole plan.

I gave him my shirt, and a few bucks for coffee. And he gave me hugs, stories of his dreams, and, at the end of the day, a big smile. He filled my heart. It was a good trade.

15

Taking Time to Grieve

Life has a way of reminding us to take care of ourselves and to do what is important in our lives.

July seems to be a month of special events and celebrations. The reverberations of June graduations, and a catching up on birthdays, weddings and funerals has filled my calendar. Covid had slowed down and often stopped those familiar rituals and life events that really are essential to our community life and our emotional wellbeing. Now, we have social calendars again and I find myself busy with those special events, events I used to take for granted, or thought that they were old-fashioned, and could be forgotten.

This week, I went to a funeral of a good friend and colleague from work. Her funeral was delayed for a year, as she wanted people to gather to celebrate her life, and not to be overcome by mourning. Then, the pandemic delayed that event for another two years.

Part of me was thinking that having a funeral now was unnecessary. Enough time had gone by that we didn't really need a funeral or even a gathering. We were "past all that" and had moved on. If my thinking was likened to a baseball game, I'd be batting a complete strikeout.

It was a serious and meaningful event, a military funeral at a national cemetery, complete with an honor guard, the firing of rifles, and the playing of "Taps". The folding and presentation of the national flag to her daughter "on behalf of the President" and in recognition of her military service might seem a little dramatic, almost a cliche. But tears rolled down my cheeks. We each had one of her favorite roses, and we shared stories of her life and her many contributions and devotion to her family, friends, and community.

Grief poured out of me and tears fell, and I joined everyone else in the laughter and crying over wonderful stories, rich memories of a life well lived. No, it wasn't "too late" to have a funeral, it wasn't too late to gather to remember a good person and good times. We all cried, and we all healed. We continued our story telling over a late breakfast, her favorite meal, at one of her favorite restaurants. Good memories came to life and when I left, I knew that I'd been able to celebrate her life and to grieve her death, and do that essential work of the soul along with many friends and her family.

A number of years ago, I was asked to be part of a memorial for a friend who had passed nearly ten years earlier. Family and friends had struggled with this friend's death, and many issues and emotions had become stuck, with no ceremony or gathering to release the complex array of feelings.

It has been said that grief is what happens when there's no place for the love to go. I understand that wisdom a lot more these days, as I am learning that I need to take the time for self-care, for community care, and to fully and wholeheartedly allow myself to mourn, to grieve, and to release some of the challenging feelings and emotions that come when a loved one dies. In any relationship, there are thoughts unsaid, feelings unexpressed when someone dies, and what is left does need to go somewhere, needs to be said.

Often, I'm not sure what that is, what words there are to describe what lies deep in my heart. Time helps me understand what is buried deep inside, so that what needs to eventually come out and be spoken and released can find its way through the complicated jumble of emotions that are tied into the knots of grief and loss. Anger is certainly involved. There are other things, too, needing to be expressed by words we find difficult to find, let alone emerge from our throats in the midst of tears.

I do know that when I cry, that when I can allow myself to find release, and to say what is on my heart, then peace is close by. I become unstuck, able to find some liberation and comfort in the work of grieving well. Some would call that detoxifying yourself, a cleansing.

After that long delayed memorial service many years ago, a number of people were able to heal, able to move on and find some understanding, some reconciliation. I found I had some unresolved grief inside of me, too, and it was past time to let that go. The memory of the departed one became more inspiring, more comforting, and people became more accepting of her work in the community as a healer, a reconciler, and a person who could inspire fundamental change in people's lives. There were many good stories told at that memorial, stories that had been locked up in grieving hearts, love that had no place to go for a while. There was a lot less self-judgment and self-blaming. Grieving well does that for each of us, and for the community.

Now, when I feel a need to go to a funeral, or to write some kind words of comfort to those experiencing loss and grief, I listen to that voice inside of me, knowing that taking that kind of affirmative action and work not only helps others and helps the community, but it helps me be a more caring and decent person, less burdened with love that has no place to go.

16

Recharging

A rainy Sunday has turned into a time of recharging. The cat is in her usual place, snoozing through the afternoon, replenishing herself for the evening forays and gearing up to remind us of her dinner time. She is, perhaps, our resident chaplain, leading us by example to recharge and renew ourselves.

Batteries for several of my electronic devices sit in their chargers. Tomorrow, the electric weedwhacker will be put to use, bringing order to my sister in law's yard. And, the camera battery will be tasked in photographing this fall's amazing display of foliage.

The earth itself is recharging, after a hectic summer. The lawn is slowly turning green from the welcome rain. Mushrooms are emerging where only a few weeks ago, the dead grass crunched and the ground was more like oven-fired clay. Even the raspberries have put out a new, unexpected crop, adding yet another layer of winter delights to the freezer. The final round of crops from the garden finish their ripening, spread around the house, as we all prepare for winter.

The garden cycle continues, as I add leaves, grass clippings and the kitchen compost bucket offerings to the compost maker. Its resident earthworms are happily overwhelmed with new-found abundance.

I plant new garlic cloves, knowing that next summer will bring abundant fresh garlic to summer vegetable stir fries and pickles. I enjoy the garlic growing to not only satisfy my love of garlic, but also because garlic is a rebel, wanting to be planted in fall and harvested in early summer, out of kilter with the other crops. A new crop in the garden, filling the spaces left open by harvest, is my celebration of hope for the future, and sparks the making of my new wish list for next year's garden.

The neighboring farmers are recharging, too. They've finished their corn harvests, followed quickly by new harrowing and the planting of their winter grass crops. What was once an experiment in planting for local farmers has now turned into part of a year-round planting and harvesting cycle. New ideas are becoming popular with the agricultural community. I am told this variety of grass adds nitrogen, protects the soil from the pounding of the winter rains, and is another food source for cows. I celebrate my neighbors' curiosity and willingness to be innovative. That spirit of curiosity, boldness, and scientific curiosity serves the community well, and inspires me to live more like a farmer.

The quiet morning stillness and the first sounds of raindrops from the incoming front offer me renewal and space in my life for some gratitude and peace. The natural cycles of this place call us out to pay attention, to take a breath and pause. As the earth recharges, as I recharge, I seek to follow that example, readying myself for new ideas, and new perspectives in this time of challenge and change.

17

The Unexpected Conversation

An often uncelebrated benefit of living in a small town s the seemingly random and unplanned conversations that occur at the grocery store or the post office.

A recent encounter at the post office turned into a deep and motivating conversation about how we help others by offering words of motivation and guidance. We shared the thought that just a plain "paying attention" talk with someone who is struggling is sometimes life changing.

"It is just as simple as a few kind words, and some gentle expectation that someone can better themselves," my friend said.

Small town life allows us to have these deep conversations, often with people we haven't been connected to. That post office sidewalk conversation allowed both of us to share commonalities, to be better friends.

"I don't have time for this?" I can say to myself. But, isn't a small contribution to some social peace, to a person's wellbeing worth a few minutes of my time? Checking off my "to do" list really isn't all that important. Maybe the list needs a line item for "care for others today".

What is our true work? Isn't it nurturing the connections, weaving the fabric of community, the offering of support and comfort? I'm often overwhelmed by the rips and tears in the social cloth, the diseases of loneliness, despair, indifference, and depression. We often see the symptoms, yet often don't focus on working on the cures. The remedies, the prescriptions for civil betterment are all around us, and it doesn't take a rocket scientist to access those and apply them to the maladies that are right in front of our faces.

Time, concern, relationship, and empathy are all in our first aid kits. We can be listeners and cheerleaders. Our life experiences have given us the knowledge and the tools to help others. We often forget what we know and what we can do to bind up the wounds of others, and to bring them into the heart of the community.

I can make time for these side conversations, the casual encounters. Those moments are often the treasures of the day, the gold in my life. If I don't make the time to stop and chat, I'm cheating myself. I'm missing out on what could be a life changing encounter, or experiencing the germination of profound ideas. Isn't that worth ten minutes of my time?

It is a two-way street. Often, that casual encounter, that deepening of connection, boosts me, becoming part of my self-care plan for the day, opening up a door to help me move ahead on a problem, to grow as a person. Looking back on life, I often see the beginning of the needed change, the fresh insight, started with a few words on the street corner or the grocery store aisle.

Someone cared about me and stopped to talk, changing my life.

I'm a believer that encounters and good conversations are usually not random, but an essential piece of the work of the Universe to bring us together, in a place where the sparks can fly and fresh ideas can take off. At the post office, I mailed a letter, picked up my mail, and deepened a relationship with a friend. My task today is to pay attention, and to give space to allow that to happen, to be willing to grow. And, to be a force for change and healing, both for myself and the community.

18

Roundabout: Struggling With Addiction

I sometimes find myself stuck, just moving in circles and not moving ahead. I like to solve problems and work a solution. Yet, life too often finds me stuck in a roundabout, unable to get off and move onto the road that leads to a satisfying resolution.

We took a road trip recently, needing to get away, and enjoy the colors of fall, and have an adventure. It was time for new perspectives.

Traveling on unfamiliar roads and through unfamiliar towns and cities, we came across a number of traffic circles. Roundabouts challenge me and I have to concentrate on my destination and the next link in the day's travels, in order to escape the circle and go on my way. My town doesn't have a roundabout, though the idea would improve the local traffic flow. I'm left with experiencing a roundabout on only an occasional basis, not enough to become comfortable, let alone an expert.

A traffic circle doesn't let me easily stop and contemplate my next move. I'm compelled to join the fray, find the correct lane and get out at the right time. It is not unusual for me to stay in the circle for a complete circle or even two, until I figure out my path of escape. Like the rest of life, it often seems to be more chaos than order.

Yet, it is efficient. Once I figure out the methodology of it all, and know my destination, I do just fine.

I have to deal with roundabouts in other ways, though, in working through the problems of life and navigating challenging relationships. Community meetings and gatherings with friends and loved ones often challenge me. I tend to stand back and watch. I pick up on the examples of old, often expected behaviors and the old ghosts of dysfunction and family dramas from past generations, the stuff that continues to be toxic for the newest generations.

We can learn and change, but sometimes, we seem to be stuck on the dysfunctional roundabout and don't know how to get off, how to leave the circle. We often repeat the toxicity of the past, and don't manage to move on.

I find the challenges of alcohol at social events to be a life-long challenge for me. Recently, I had some deep conversations with two members of the generation behind me, men I've often encouraged and counseled, as they've struggled in their lives, often plagued by their wounds and addictions. Alcohol is their poison of choice, how they self-medicate to try to kill their pain of rejections, abandonments, and challenges with self-esteem and appreciation for deep down goodness and compassion. They are good men, and when you scrape away the drunkenness and self-anger, they are loving and compassionate.

I haven't talked with them in a state of sobriety for at least the last twenty years. I struggle with making the effort, with sitting down with them, and going deep about the meaning of life, of self-respect. Being the good role model, the wise elder is a challenging role for me to play as they pound down the first dozen of their day's beers.

Still, I make the effort, I have the conversations, and I try to keep the gate open with them, trying to build our relationship. I strive to be the good bridge keeper, a healer of some of our more challenging issues. I keep hoping the day will soon come when they reach out to me, telling me they want to get sober, and invite me into that work. I keep hoping to find my magic wand, yet I know that true sobriety, true insight begins when they, and not me, decide it is time for change.

Until then, our relationship is stuck in a roundabout, circling around the hard conversations, the long histories of trauma, abuse, neglect, and chaos, the stuff that one tries so desperately to ignore, the challenges you try to drown with your beer. We circle, we change lanes sometimes, but we're often stuck and don't seem to know how to break that circle, and move on with our lives and our relationships.

Each of us can break our generational curses, our guilt and shame. We can begin our own traditions, expectations of friendship and be free.

I want to think that I really do have a magic wand. It isn't covered with fairy dust, and it doesn't instantly solve worries and problems that have festered for generations. My magic wand involves time and patience, and unconditional love. It involves a belief that people truly can change, that each of us can dig deep and learn about ourselves and our wounds, that we have the tools in hand to take on and deal with a lifetime of worries and stress. We can change, each of us. Change and the rest of our lives can begin with one step in the right direction, and having the support of someone who loves us, who can hold our hand, and who believes that we are worthy of that effort to move ahead.

My job in all this is to be the good friend, the patient one, offering myself as an example of a different path, and to offer my unconditional love and compassion to them. I'm old enough to know that preaching and condemning builds even higher walls, and doesn't provide the answers that will come, eventually. I need to wait, and I keep extending my hand in friendship and love, trying to be that friend that is always there, always caring, and always representing the alternative path, the way out of the seemingly endless circles of addiction and self-destruction.

Perhaps these conversations have pushed open some doors, making the path to sobriety and insight just a little more easy to find. Perhaps they have heard and felt my love for them, and that life offers some choices, that there is a way out of the real traffic circles of our lives.

19

Being the Healer: What Am I Here For

We are all healers," the noted epidemiologist stated, as he spoke at a recent webinar on the scientific research on Covid. The webinar involved highly intelligent, experienced and thoughtful people. A former president, governors of large states inundated with this crisis, thoughtful medical and other scientifically trained experts and thinkers were the lineup of speakers. The conversations were rich, insightful, as well as comforting to me. Intelligent people were working on these problems, developing approaches and methodologies, being rational and thoughtful.

In one segment, a panel of epidemiological experts gathered, and I was expecting profound wisdom on viruses, containment, the search for the "cure". What is the most important thing each of us can do was the question posed?

"We are all healers," one of the experts said. "Making a human connection with someone else is the most profound, the most effective act we can take in dealing with these problems."

Another expert added that taking five minutes to deeply, intensely listen to someone, to spend that small amount of time focused on another person's thoughts and concerns, is profound and highly effective.

I was expecting to hear of ground-breaking medical analysis, maybe the development of a miracle drug, or some other scientific discovery. Instead, I heard words about kindness and interpersonal relationships being the key factors in treatment and remedies.

Their answers weren't looking at the intricacies of public health strategies or developing new scientific approaches and techniques, though the webinar participants did speak to those vital actions. Those steps are important and ongoing. Yet, we were reminded that the most important thing we bring to any situation, any crisis, is our humanity.

Being kind, attentive, and being focused on the needs and concerns of another human being, making that very human, intimate connection, does the most to change the situation, to empower each of us, and to bring about meaningful change. All the medicine, the technology, the social change actions that are coming forward now, that's all important. But, not as important as our task to be compassionate, to be loving, to be caring, and to simply and intensely focus on what we all need and want, to be cared about, to be valued as a person, to be deeply loved.

The words took me aback, made me pause. Are scientists now thinking that our humanity, our compassion, is an essential scientifically appropriate remedy?

Throughout this crisis, I have been asking myself, what can I do? What is my role here?

After all, it is a time to be involved, to add myself in as a responder, as a caregiver, as part of the solution. That is what citizens do in time of societal chaos and challenge. We step up to the plate, take on a task we are good at, and move ahead with others for the common good.

"We are all healers."

"Be the compassionate deep listener."

"Be a 'communitarian'."

Ah, the word of the year, this "communitarian". Caring about and being part of the community, being focused on our role as humanitarians living together.

This crisis again calls us to think of ourselves as citizens of the world. We are so very interconnected. Our collective ability to weave our economic, educational, and cultural lives together throughout the planet is one of the profound lessons of today. The good that we do, and the destructive consequences of that interconnectedness that makes this pandemic so destructive, and so universal, offer lessons in that interconnectedness. We are truly reliant upon each other which is such a big part of our lives now. We are world citizens, and we are very interdependent with each other.

The transmission of the virus shows that interconnectedness, and that we are all affected by how everyone else, even one person, thinks and acts.

The scientific evidence of global climate change has been compelling and strong, yet many of our actions and our thinking has not really changed because we tend to not think that taking small steps to ensure a healthier, more productive outcome will really make a difference.

This pandemic is teaching us otherwise. Avoiding crowds, practicing social distancing, and staying home avoids contagion and literally saves lives. Simple steps can be highly effective, if we all act together, coming together as one force, one movement towards a safer world.

This lesson has been lost to us, but now it has become real, taught to us in the daily statistics of illness and death. The pandemic has forced us to pay attention, and to learn some basic life-altering lessons.

It is all on me. That's where this conversation comes back to. I can watch the news, sitting in my living room, passive and inactive. At the end of the day, I've accomplished nothing. I am not being the active citizen, nor am I being true to my own morals and ethics, my own purpose in life.

Yet I am a healer, a listener, and I can impact the lives of those around me. That's what we can all do, to act locally, to be the change agent with those around us.

I live in a community. I want to be a humanitarian, a communitarian. I am a builder, a healer. And, that starts with me, here and now, right now.

20

Adapting to Change

I wrote this after a particularly heated and divisive election season.

The quiet you are hearing today as you sip your coffee is the resuming of normal life after the frantic election season. The political advertising noise is fading into the past, and one can collect their thoughts without being bombarded, manipulated, and offered endless rides on the roller coasters of political hype. I'm still trying to burn off the adrenaline and angst that the marketers and a number of my friends and neighbors have been firing up in our community life.

It might even be safe to have coffee with a friend and exchange pleasantries at the grocery store and post office, without needing to evaluate if your encounter and your comments will further escalate tensions and social anxiety.

No matter what the election returns mean to each of us, we still live in our community. We still have family, friends, and neighbors who we value. We are still together, and we still share our lives, our hopes, and our dreams. I still want to believe that the vast majority of us are good people, who are living their lives with compassion and a determination to make a better world.

Life goes on.

No matter who received the most votes, our community issues are still here, and still need our attention. We still have work to do. Not necessarily political work, mind you, but vital work nonetheless.

We have work to do with having safe and loving relationships, our work, raising kids, and being in community. Those concerns don't go away just because we have an election. And, hopefully the campaigns focused some much-needed attention on the needs of those less fortunate and better ways that we can all address the many concerns we have as a community and as good citizens.

Yes, the act of voting is an important work that we do as citizens. I'm heartened that this election brought a high turnout, and people participated and expressed their viewpoints. There was no shortage of opinions, issues, and public policy choices on the ballot. A democratic society, with often loud expressions of opinions, many debates, and lively conversations, isn't very neat and orderly. Democracy is not easy, and carrying out the duties of citizenship can test our patience. Yet, the conversations are opportunities to be better informed and to perhaps challenge some of our opinions and deeply held values.

Those conversations will continue and will bear fruit, without the high drama and angst of a national election.

It is time to take a collective breath and remind ourselves that we live in this community together, that we each contribute to the common good, that each of our opinions are important. Elections and political discussions are just part of what makes our community a special and cherished place to live and grow our families and friendships.

The other, quieter work is what is back on our collective agendas today. Life goes on, opinions may still differ, and we will continue to grow and make a better world.

As the election news slowly quiets down, I sip my coffee and enjoy the beauty of the season. We've earned some down time, some solitude and contemplation. It is a time of healing and reflection on who we are, and where we are going.

The election may have stirred up our differences, and our passions on who should be our leaders and where we are going as a country. Yet, we really are the same people as we were before the election: good people with fundamentally charitable and kindly values, people who are more than capable of building a better community and country. I remind myself that, despite our differences, we have more in common than our disagreements, that we have shared values, hopes and dreams. Together we are stronger, and we are moving forward.

This week's election brought yet another wave of change in a year that has become a symbol of life being unsettled, routines disrupted, and a continual parade of adaptations to change. We are inundated with new information and changes in how we navigate our lives and live in society.

We awaken to political changes, both in who holds public office and adopts public policies, to new laws adopted by the voters. Our economy and social lives continually adapt to developments in medical science dealing with a pandemic that, as of October, 2022, has killed over a million Americans, sickened nearly another 100 million, and ravaged the world's economies, health and transportation. We haven't begun to really understand what those numbers mean to our lives and our national psychology.

What was normal a year ago is often only memories, as we try to navigate our way by wearing masks, social distancing, and shutting down entire sectors of our economy. Virtual learning and internet meetings are the new normal, with continual change being one of the few constants in this new world. We are challenged in new ways and are called upon to be flexible, and adapt to the new normal, except life now is anything but normal.

Thomas Jefferson expressed his views on change over two hundred years ago, writing:

"I am not an advocate for frequent changes in laws and constitutions, but laws and institutions must go hand in hand with the progress of the human mind. As that becomes more developed, more enlightened, as new discoveries are made, new truths discovered and manners and opinions change, with the change of circumstances, institutions must advance also to keep pace with the times. We might as well require a man to wear still the coat which fitted him when a boy as civilized society to remain ever under the regimen of their barbarous ancestors."

Today, the pace of the need to change is often breathtaking and overwhelming.

How do I cope? How do I navigate through all these changes, almost all of them being out of my control and certainly not on my list of what I would like to see in my life. Many days,

I feel at a loss on how to manage my life, let alone feel a sense of predictability and normality in daily life.

Today is different than yesterday, and tomorrow will have even more new experiences and requirements. I often feel I can't keep up, I can't manage my life, that life would be better if I could just stay in bed and pull a blanket over my head.

We Americans, however, are an adaptable lot. We go with the flow, we accommodate, and we adapt. We are good at learning something new and making change work for us. We see change as an opportunity and a challenge to grow. We often choose to see the change as an opportunity rather than an obstacle.

"How can I make this work for me?" Can I leverage this challenge as an asset, seeing the glass as half full rather than half empty, a benefit rather than a disaster?

If my candidate or a ballot measure I've taken an interest in falls short at the polls, is there a way to response, to move forward, and still advance my values, still give me a place in the community forum? Are my ideas and my values still meritorious? Should I continue to pursue them and hope to be more persuasive in this new era?

Or should I be more thoughtful, more critical, taking the political loss as an opportunity to re-evaluate, reassess my position. Do I need more evidence, do I need a better argument, should I consider the opposition's viewpoints as healthy and constructive criticism?

Or perhaps there is merit on differing points of view, that out of the debate, there can be a meeting of the minds, a spirit of compromise, or at least the recognition that there are valid points of view on the issue or the candidate. Out of that process of education, evaluation and weighing of ideas, new ideas can emerge, and there can be some collective agreement, perhaps even compromise.

We can move on. We can perhaps agree that the campaigns have been educational, intellectually stimulating and have aired a challenging issue. Those clashes of ideas have strengthened our knowledge and have enabled us to build a more united focus on important issues. More accurately defining an issue and spotlighting different opinions may bring clarity to tough subjects, and we become more articulate debaters. Redefining the question may be the most valuable outcome of a heated campaign.

Yet, let's not wait for someone else to lead the way, to put us back on the road to a healthy, progressive outlook on life and national problem-solving. Each of us is part of the solution, and the time to begin that healing work is now.

21

Wanting Change: How Does That Happen?

Often, I react to the news with despair, anger and frustration. I remind myself that the "news" is often sensationalized, that the news business is a business, and that almost all the "good news" is not included in a news program. Yet, what much of what is "news" stirs me up to wanting change, a different approach to old problems.

If I want change, I have to act.

If I am passive, then others will make changes, or not. And those actions or inactions will likely not be what I want to see happen. I will not have a voice. My silence, my inaction diminishes my soul and my purpose in life. I can be part of the solution. That is my choice.

"You must be the change you want to see in the world," Mahatma Gandhi famously said.

Yet, to borrow a phrase from Al Gore, it is an inconvenient truth.

If I don't like what I read in the news, then either I am an instrument to change the world, or I do nothing. My inaction assures that I lose my right to express my disagreement with what is going on. After all, actions speak louder than words.

I am in charge of how I react and respond, how I am an instrument of change, putting action into my beliefs, and thus creating change, building a better world.

If I don't like what I see in my community, my neighborhood, my family, then I need to step up and get involved, and become an instrument of change.

A healthier community starts with me. Put up or shut up. It's all on me.

The simple acts are the easiest and the most effective. They have the greatest impact long term.

Here's a list of actions for me, and, hopefully, you:

- Invite a friend to coffee.
- Play music, and teach someone else, sharing music with others, creating joy and community.
- Start a conversation with a stranger.
- Send an inspirational note or story to a friend.
- Reach out to a prisoner, someone who is going through a hard patch, someone in pain.
- Acknowledge someone's loss, or a challenge, and offer them a compliment, a few words of cheer and encouragement. They are not alone.
- Practice patience and understanding.
- Don't expect a reward or recognition. Acting anonymously can be very sweet.

- Practice forgiveness and compassion, even if another's words or acts seem hurtful.
- Imagine walking in the shoes of another.
- Remember the Greek proverb: "A society grows great when old men plant trees whose shade they shall never sit in."
- Slow to judge, quicker to forgive.
- Intend to follow the Golden Rule.
- Examine your own biases and prejudices. Do some personal housekeeping. I've found this to be very humbling and enlightening.
- Suspend judgement.
- Don't assume.

My ego gets in the way in this work, but if I am honest, I learn more about myself and the world, and I move forward to be a better human being.

And, the world changes, just a little.

22

Unexpected Gifts: Giving From the Heart

Putting aside the hubbub, the seemingly endless demands on us to be "in the holiday mode", I find my purpose and comfort in the quiet of the winter, as I contemplate what are the best gifts to exchange.

The birds quietly chatter their thanks as I fill their feeder. The rest of the yard sleeps, as a few leaves, still dressed in their fall colors, cling to the branches. These moments are gifts to my spirit, and are given freely, without expectation.

The chance encounters in life can offer the best experiences, the most rewarding gift giving of the season.

While on a welcome road trip last week, I stopped for lunch. While pouring my coffee, the waitress mentioned her struggle with her trembling hand. I took the time to listen. I recently came across an article that talked about that condition and a new non-invasive and pain free treatment. In a few minutes, our phones connected and she had the link to the article and the contact for the competent, state of the art clinic that could ease her condition.

"I didn't know about this. And I so badly want to be able to paint and draw again," she said.

She gave me a big smile as I left, her relief at finding a solution showing in her eyes, her gift to me.

I've lost touch with a fellow guitar player. While playing one of his favorite songs the other day, I decided he needed a gift. I've come across some unusual picks that suit my continuing journey to be a better guitar player. I had a few extra picks, so I mailed them to him, with a note thanking him for his friendship over the years.

I'm sure the postal clerk wondered why I had a big smile as I mailed that package.

Often, the best gifts to give are the gifts of listening and appreciation. There are so many opportunities to simply be present with someone, to listen with an open heart, and to suspend judgment and commentary. Most of us aren't asking for advice; we simply want to be heard.

"To be by their side," a counselor friend told me the other day. "It truly is the gift we can all give. All it takes is our time and being present with someone in need of a good ear."

We all have our story, but all too often, our story doesn't get heard. That's all too often the gift we need to receive, as well as to give.

When we prepare for the holidays and wrap our presents, perhaps we should write a kind note to a friend, inviting them for a cup of coffee or a walk in a beautiful place. Let us suspend our culture's pressure to give material things. Instead, we can give the gift of ourselves and our open, loving hearts.

23

Happiness

It comes into my life in many ways, so often in the most simple, ordinary ways. Events and experiences, often simple observations of what seems to be ordinary, but warms my heart and lights up my soul.

Happiness is all around us, and comes into our lives by the simple act of being aware, of observing, often just noticing.

Happiness can come from friends, in many ways, often unexpected. Like friendship, happiness is intangible, defying measure and study. It just appears in our lives, if we take the time to notice it, and let it come inside of us. Often, it is already there, deep inside of us, and we need to observe, breathe it in and observe.

The postal clerk brought me happiness the other day, wrapped in an ordinary, brown padded envelope. My friend's name was on the envelope, without a clue to the contents of this unexpected delivery. It was Christmas Eve, yet I wasn't expecting a gift from my friend. He's a generous soul, a man with a big heart and a kindly person. His talents are many, yet he is always hesitant about talking about all that he can do, and all that he can create.

His modesty about his accomplishments often hides his potential and his gift to teach and guide others in their lives. He's shy and soft-spoken, yet when we have a deep conversation, his deep knowledge and extensive thought on the topic always offers insight and wisdom. He'll deny all of that, being his humble self. His abilities and deep thinking can be buried deep, but emerge like bright rays of the rising sun, when the conversation opens up and he feels comfortable in being able to express what is in his heart.

Good friends are like that, our infrequent face to face conversations so often pick up where they left off, months or even years apart.

I tore open the envelope, and two amazing creations slide out onto my lap. Hand crafted, leather, metal snaps, several braided cords. Shiny, well-finished leather straps, and an amazingly clever cinch bag of soft suede. Delicate, precise stitching, hand-punched holes for the threads, each stitch and knot precise, exact, and lovingly made. Created especially for me.

It was art and functionality and love, all in an amazing creation. The hand-tooled Japanese writing symbol, a kanji, graced the outer bottom of each bag. I did not know its meaning, but I suspected it was Japanese. I knew my friend had been a student of the Japanese language, and was also a student of Zen and Buddhist thought. I reached out to another friend, who lives in Tokyo and, by his choice of domicile, is also a student of Japanese culture and language. Through the miracles of the internet, that friend soon provided me with the translation. Again, my friend gives to me more than once, enabling me to reconnect with another friend, and to share the joy of his gift with yet another. My friend is the master of modeling how pay it forward, to being kind and generous.

Of course, what a great choice of a word for such a gift. The giver of this gift knew that I play guitar, an interest we share. Though, he is a much more intuitive and accomplished. A number of years ago, when we began our friendship, we were able to spend some time together in person, and he was a great teacher with his guitar with me and with others.

The two bags are perfect for the storing of guitar picks, and are to be tied to the headstock of one's guitar, providing both storage and an additional beautiful accessory to one's guitar. I have a number of guitars, yet the bags are being placed on my two favorites. The dangling bag occasionally touches the hand that fingers the chords, allowing the player to feel its presence. For me, when I play, the spirit and kindness of my friend will always be with me, a way to feel his presence and his spiritual guidance, and his profound kindness and generosity.

Happiness

Gratitude. How do I express my gratitude for such kindness? My friend would counsel me to pay it forward, to be kind and generous to others.

Happiness. These gifts are happiness embodied, coming to life for me, giving me a reminder of his gift of friendship, his love for music, and his deep kind soul.

24

Simple Gifts

Near the end of the year, the holidays are upon us, with the usual seasonal barrage of promotions, sales, Black Friday, and an e-mail inbox overflowing with all of those special deals. Bargains galore! A good part of me recoils and rebels from such marketing and promotion. In reality, I really have quite enough "stuff". And the real pleasures come from time with friends and some peaceful contemplation in the company of some candlelight.

We recently visited a big box store, needing to replace a laptop that had finally died. The aisles were overflowing with at least several hundred flat screen TVs that had somehow managed to get through the supply chain bottlenecks, so they could now effectively clutter up the aisles at the giant store.

Surely there aren't that many people who have that item at the top of their holiday wish list. I wondered out loud if Americans really need even more flat screen TVs. Can't you only watch one at a time, and, by now, there have been enough TVs sold so people can have one in every room? Not that I think that there's all that much being broadcast or streamed that is all that worthy of my time and attention.

I'm reminded of the old hymn, *Simple Gifts*, its lyrics clearly calling us back to reflect on the "reason for the season". The song isn't in the Christmas song books, but maybe it should be.

"'Tis the gift to be simple, 'tis the gift to be free,
'Tis the gift to come down where we ought to be,
And when we find ourselves in the place just right,
'Twill be in the valley of love and delight.
When true simplicity is gain'd,
To bow and to bend we will not be asham'd,
To turn, turn will be our delight,
Till by turning, turning we come round right."

This year, I've shortened my own "wish list", realizing after all of our pandemic time of reducing the frenzy of modern life, that the simple things are really the best. Quiet, reflective time, time over coffee with a good friend, a walk in the sunshine, or listening to the murmurs of rain on a walk in a peaceful place.

I've sorted through some of the stuff that often clutters up my life. I'm giving a cherished family heirloom to my niece, so she and her kids can retell the story of how the ancestors brought the chair over the Oregon Trail, tying it to the back of the covered wagon, and how it occupied my grandmother's living room, in a place of honor and storytelling. I've retold that story enough now and it's time for a new generation to have that pleasure. And I think Grandma would be happy with that.

The added bonus with that gift giving is a road trip and family time, as well as the passing on of some memories to people who will appreciate it.

I'll still write my Christmas cards and send out a newsy, perhaps hokey, letter to friends and family I connect with only a few times a year. I could substitute those sentiments via an e-mail or blog post, but don't we enjoy holding a letter from a friend while enjoying a cup of tea on a rainy afternoon? And, I like the ritual of addressing the envelopes and sticking on the Santa stamps. I'll probably stir up some Christmas fudge and a batch of cookies, savoring the memories of doing that with family who have long since departed this world, walking down memory lane with some time-worn recipes.

But I don't need much more than that. A few walks under the downtown Christmas lights, and a cheery concert or two of holiday classics will gladden my heart, without the need for dealing with the mobs on Black Friday.

It is a simple time, celebrating simple things, simple gifts like friendship, caring for others, and just enjoying the simple pleasures of the holidays.

25

Epilogue

"To laugh often and much; to win the respect of intelligent people and the affection of children. To earn the appreciation of honest critics and endure the betrayal of false friends; to appreciate beauty, to find the best in others; to leave the world a bit better, whether by a healthy child, a garden patch well-tended or a redeemed social condition; to know even one life has breathed easier because you have lived. This is to have succeeded."

--Ralph Waldo Emerson

ACKNOWLEDGEMENTS

I am grateful to my wife, Karen Keltz, who is my strong advocate and motivator, continually urging me to "get your ideas out there". Her advice and encouragement is, as always, invaluable. To my friends and acquaintances throughout my life, who are always continual encouragers and motivators. To the ever hard working and cheerful crew at my favorite coffee shop, who have continually inquired what I am working on, and hoping to see the results of their countless cups of coffee. And, to the many people I've come across whose acts of kindness and charity continue to inspire me, and who are the inspiration, the heart, and the soul for this work.

Neal C. Lemery

Neal Lemery is a community volunteer, focused on energizing his community and people who care about the future of our youth and the vitality of organizations that strive to better family life and the web of community life.

The author of four books and a long list of essays and feature stories about mentoring and community caretakers and activists, Lemery draws on his experiences as a small town lawyer, prosecutor and judge, as well as a lifetime of being actively engaged in community life. He continues to mentor and advocate for the underprivileged, the neglected, and the voiceless.

Lemery wrote his first book, *Mentoring Boys to Men: Climbing Their Own Mountains*, to share his experiences and to encourage others to pay attention to the plight of a lost generation of young men. Readers urged him to share more stories and to expand his work on advocating for real change and new opportunities for the youth that our society has left behind.

He brings new energy and ideas to one of his favorite quotes, "Be the change you want to see in the world." –Mahatma Gandhi

CPSIA information can be obtained
at www.ICGtesting.com
Printed in the USA
LVHW080326241222
735796LV00030B/677